Pre-level

CHOMP!
Big Teeth

Ruth A. Musgrave

DK

Some teeth are big.
Some are small.
These teeth will make
you smile.

These deer
have two
long teeth.

Chinese water deer

This big cat
has sharp teeth.

clouded leopard

Look at how these teeth stick out!

babirusa

[BA-buh-roo-sa]

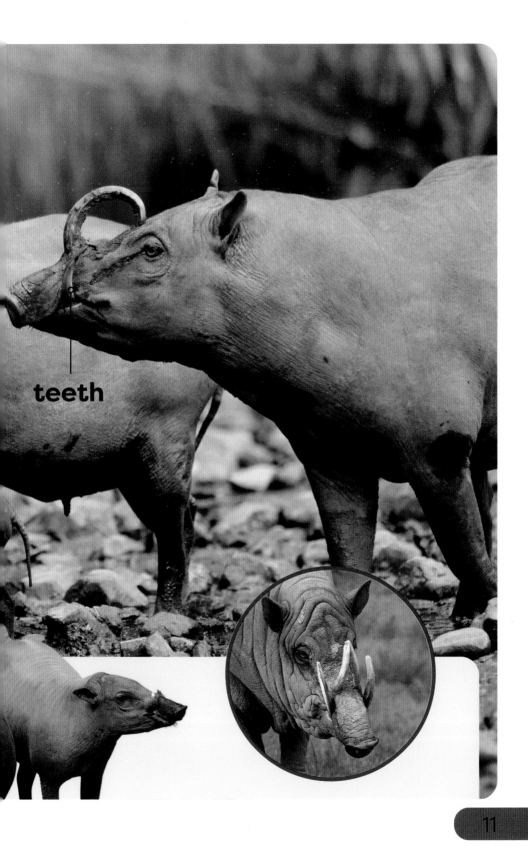

teeth

An otter opens shells with its teeth.
It eats the meat inside.

sea otter

This animal digs holes with its teeth.

naked mole rat

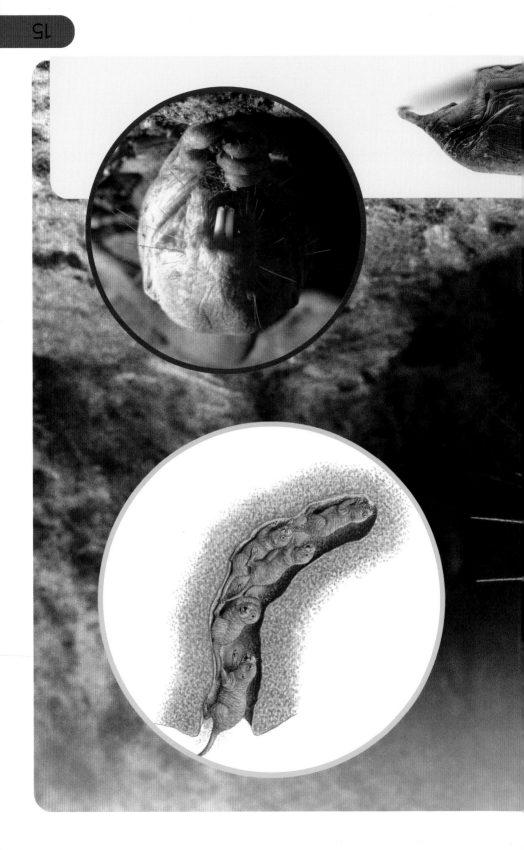

beaver

This animal
cuts down trees.
It makes a house
with sticks.

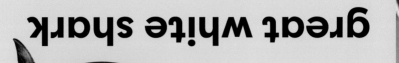

great white shark

This animal eats fish.
It has many rows
of teeth.

Open wide!
Mom has big teeth.
Her baby will, too,
when it grows up.

hippopotamus

This animal
grabs food
with its teeth.

crocodile

This animal lives
in the cold.
It uses its teeth to get
out of the water.

walrus

These teeth
can pull off
tree bark.

elephant

This animal has the longest tooth of all.

narwhal

[NAR-wall]

Animals need teeth.
They use them to eat
and stay safe.
Now that's something
to smile about.

Glossary

crocodile
an animal that lives
in water

naked mole rat
an animal that digs
and lives in the dirt

great white shark
a fish that lives in
the ocean

hippopotamus
an animal that lives in
the water and eats
grass on land

narwhal
a whale that lives where
it is cold

Quiz

Answer the questions to see what you have learned. Check your answers with an adult.

1. How does an otter use its teeth?

2. Which animal digs with its teeth?

3. Which animal has many rows of teeth?

4. Which animal pulls bark off a tree?

5. Which animal has the longest tooth?

1. To open shells 2. Naked mole rat 3. Great white shark
4. Elephant 5. Narwhal